Royal Blue Shutters

by Lisa Brognano

Fernwood
PRESS

Royal Blue Shutters

©2022 by Lisa Brognano

Fernwood Press
Newberg, Oregon
www.fernwoodpress.com

Printed in the United States of America

Cover and page design: Mareesa Fawver Moss

Cover image: Sarah Dorweiler via Unsplash

ISBN 978-1-59498-085-5

Library of Congress Control Number: 2022936033

For Nanno with the mustache, artist and old world carpenter, and the great-grandmother I resemble (although she had two inches on me and lived beneath Mount Etna), my lovely little Nanni who wore hand-sewn dresses to compliment her silver hair and warm smile, Nanno Charles in all the photographs looking so dashing, and of course for our sweet Aunt Martha who thought of my sisters and me as daughters: you were the creatives, the handsome men and beautiful ladies, unfettered by fear, grown in hard work and love—

And for my husband, James—my one and only—the big, strong man who gives me so much joy!

Foreword

In the South, many homeowners paint their doors, porch ceilings, and shutters blue. It is a common sight with origins dating back to enslaved people with roots from central and West Africa. The color blue is meant to ward off agitated and easily angered spirits. The tactic was to create the appearance of water and sky.

It was believed that ghosts do not traditionally cross water. It was also believed that spirits could be tricked into crossing over to the other side if they could see heaven.

The title of this latest collection of Lisa Brognano's work, *Royal Blue Shutters*, immediately struck me as something that asked me to consider what frames the windows of my own home—this soul—and what superstitions help me create a story of protection.

It may serve to point the reader to the idea that we all put up walls, and that at times, through poetry, we create portals to help us pass through the messier parts of life—love, lust, mortality, divinity, doubt, and yearning.

It is in Lisa's poem, "Royal Blue Shutters," that this work is titled after, that she reminds us that even the best efforts to protect ourselves can be shattered by storms "that beat the land unconscious, shutters lying on the ground, split in half."

Writing poetry is an undertaking that allows us to reflect on the many events and experiences that both grieve and perplex us. Poets seek to understand our relationship with our human counterparts and nature in juxtaposition to ourselves.

There is a certain want in Lisa's work to return to the beginning, our creation story, our need to better understand Adam and Eve, to go back to our beginnings. It reverberates through her poetry. And in her poem, "Mad for Jane," she writes "or maybe she would forget/about writing and throw him down/on the bed to experience the weight of his muscles pinning her against/the covers like a leaf pressed into a book." In "Johnny and the Salt Water Tide," "ladies' legs dangled/in olive-drab waves/while hairy-chested men wandered/over to chat with them."

The division of man and woman, of stoniness and emotion, is etched out over the pages of her work in a journey to understand the gap between love and lust. In "Ivan and Tara" she writes, "Not abysmal to think/of what could have been/if the vows were put back/into their mouths, eaten and swallowed...the kind Tara found humbling/Ivan preferred to nibble, naturally."

In "From Her Diary," she reasons that "God didn't explain his reasons to me/about replanting that tree in the middle/of the garden...(that) surely, Adam tells me not to blame/myself for the events of that first day."

Our most human selves are seen in the lustful dance of nature. In "Leading Up to the Storm," we become voyeurs to the "Belching clouds jerked one way/across an attractive mauve sky,/perilously close to one another—a mating/ritual exposed to view."

She considers the "redundancy of arks" in her poem "Ark of Cross Purposes." It is here we consider Noah's Ark and the metaphor the ark brings to our own lives in an attempt to pull what is both grass-eating and flesh-eating into our own boats for saving. If we are to start over, are we to include the "jungle beast?"—beasts that also come as house-cats when in "Urbanite" she discovers that "being an analyst had its down-/sides but so did owning a cat/who didn't seem to care/for her taste in men."

It's important to return to the idea of blue, the blue of the shutters that frame the windows, that protect the inhabitants from being taken by ghosts. In the South, it is a haint blue, one made of Indigo plant that is almost a mint green that is traditionally used. Cruelly, the Indigo plant that enslaved people used to create the color only worked to further enslave them as the production of the dye "energized the 18th-century transatlantic slave trade."

In Lisa's poem, "Acquiring Sheep," there is a certain warning that even security brings risks, and if we are not aware that we are in danger of selling our soul to the devil in exchange for greed—"nevertheless, the men who grabbed/ his hand and shook it firmly/controlled each fleck's direction,/something he hadn't counted on."

But Lisa's shutters are "royal" blue. They are formal and superior; they are the color of spiritual healing. And in "Nighthawk," we are reminded of that "navy quirky sky" that "demanded her attention." The movement of the hawk, "a knowledgeable pilot/with a dinner plate on the moon" is the poet searching that sky with razor sharp precision for what nourishes.

In "Ode to Eve," Eve speaks to her daughter with authority, "Remember what I taught you, she said/and redid the braid with violet ribbons,/green leaves and amber twigs."

Christine Redman-Waldeyer, phD, is a poet, editor, and an Associate Professor of English and Journalism at Passaic County College in New Jersey. She has published several poetry collections, including: *Frame by Frame, Gravel,* and *Eve Asks*, with Muse Pie Press. Her poetry has been widely published in journals and anthologies. She is the co-editor of *Writing After Retirement* (Rowan and Littlefield, 2014) and is the founder and editor of *Adanna Literary Journal*. In 2011, she was a guest poet in residency under the Poetry Project founded by Dr. Mary Ann Miller at Caldwell College.

Introduction

The collected poems in *Royal Blue Shutters* explore the pull and tug of language, the tin-like sounds, the careful alignment, and robust admiration of words. Stanzas are bulked up with their own musicality—songs that can't be sung but only released from the lips in a prattle.

Their subject matter turns the ordinary on its head, bringing questions to the fore about what it means to take one's place on the world's unglamorous stage. Insights of rare beauty are shared as chitchat, and whether petite in nature or longer, these poems are vignettes about life's inexplicable yet dutiful rhythm.

Let me be the first to tell you the truth. I'm a wordsmith. There's a starkness to it, I'll admit. The summers of my youth were spent writing poetry and short stories—in between drawing houses on paper with markers. I'm the daughter of an architect, you see.

We eventually got a pool, which put my writing on hold for the clear, sunny days. I don't think I ever thanked Mom and Dad for leveling the ground behind the shed, the one Dad built himself, the perfect spot to squander life's toasty months. Far less complicated than the rain that brought me inside occasionally were the golden rules of summer—to splash, drink lemonade, and get tan. The consequences of a heat wave only led me to believe that school and homework were the enemies here, not that I minded the first as much as the second.

Memories such as those are as much a part of my writing as every other little thing along the way, good or bad. The creative mind absorbs wonders, oddities, and simple pleasures. Then it squeezes them out in forms that are uniquely the poet's own. Experiences and observations, for me, tend to become stamped in my mind for later use. A germination process occurs, one that may be swift or lengthy.

The concept of milking a cow is very similar. Poems well up inside and require release with a little labor. At times, there's an urgency to their expulsion but not always. As a novelist and poet, I often write verse in the summer and prose in the winter, but ideas squirt into the aluminum pail on their own schedule and not on mine.

So many poems slip away, though, especially the night-time ones that appear like heavy objects before sleep when my body and mind are relaxed. Sometimes they're perfect lines of iambic pentameter or a stanza of free verse. All I know is they don't survive until morning. Attempts to memorize every word, thinking I'm actually doing it, when, in fact, I'm nearly asleep, doesn't work. A pen and paper on the nightstand, my brilliant idea to record the flow of poetry without leaving the bed, dries inspiration up altogether. One of life's ironies, I guess.

Every poem, of course, has a skeleton underneath. Readers who dare to strip off the layers find hidden gems. Some of the revelations are author driven but not all. That might be what I like best about intention vs. interpretation. I know what I set out to create in the work, but a reader can take anything they want from the words, creating a new reality for the poem.

To write notes in the margins is one of my favorite things. Pencil scribbles everywhere mean you've unlocked a secret or two. What I intended for the reader to feel or think in no way restricts the second meaning you may glean based on your own experiences. The poems keep giving. They transform.

How words sit next to one another on the page, like folks on a public bus, intrigues me and always has. The importance of content has to be there but not above the role language plays in dressing it up. Poetry is nonfiction's pretty cousin with a great personality to match.

What I hope above all else is that you enjoy the book. Reread the poems you like and forget about those you don't. After all, the challenge of poetry is rib-sticking stuff. You want to feel full afterward.

And to clear things up, no, I didn't grow up on a farm. I was just trying to confuse you earlier. The closest reference I've got to the land and animals would be my parents' enormous garden and a cat my sisters and I had growing up.

Acknowledgments

The first time I spoke with Eric, I knew *Royal Blue Shutters* had found its perfect home. What a pleasure it's been to work with him and everyone at the press! I'd like to thank Linda, Tayve, and Art for previewing my book. Their thoughtful insights into my work are appreciated. An enormous thank you goes to Christine for writing the foreword. I can't thank her enough.

My mother speaks three languages. I only understand one of them. Her grammatical wizardry in proofing my manuscripts saves me from looking foolish. It's no wonder I value her suggestions at every step. To round out her charms, she's a phenomenal baker who outdoes herself with extra handfuls of the good stuff—chocolate morsels—in recipes that don't call for any. Treats from her oven make your mouth water. The fact that she volunteers in our community to better the lives of others accentuates how lucky I am to call her Mom.

My father can fix anything. He's the small-engine whisperer, lucky for my husband who has lots of things in need of repair. Dad makes beautiful handmade birthday cards, too. I've always loved the people he draws. If pressed to think of anything my father doesn't know something about, I'd draw a blank. Plumbing, heating, electrical, berms, swales, bicycles—he's handy to have around and awfully handsome. He even dabbled in dentistry when my sisters and I were small, pulling our loose teeth because Mom found it gross.

My eldest sister, Josie, who adored rainy days, is so special to me. Dr. Josie always looked brilliant in her lab coat. Her professional demeanor and etiquette always put everyone at ease. They knew they were in good hands. As a pianist with natural talent, we loved to hear her play the songs we could never dream of learning. Equally magnificent on the clarinet, and first chair in the high school band, it was always a delight to listen. Of course she was an A student, the classic overachiever, setting an excellent example for her little sisters. Always in service to others, she achieved a great deal in a short amount of time. We love you, Josie, with all our hearts and souls.

Maria, my older sister, makes raising two boys look easy. She can do twenty things at once and still have perfectly folded laundry, dinner on the table, lunches packed, and PTA business handled. Her colleagues miss her, as do all the teachers under her leadership as principal. I've never known anyone who takes such great care of young minds. Sometimes when we're out shopping, her former students, all grown with kids of their own, express how positively she influenced their lives and how they couldn't have risen to the same heights without her. You're my BFF, Maria!

The nephews are handsome, smart, and funny. They're growing like the weeds around the basketball court. I love to watch them swim and hit home runs all summer long. Tyler's fourteen now, and the best dressed teenager I know. Noah's right behind him at thirteen, always looking cool, too. I love being an auntie to those two. They give everything their all and aren't afraid of much. I find them both so inspiring. What young heroes!

My husband is amazing in every way. He thinks he should win the husband-of-the-year award, and sometimes I agree with him, but those ten-minute backrubs need to turn into twenty for a nomination from me! Love you, honey.

The gift of faith informs all that I do. Jesus, Mary, and Joseph, you have my perpetual thanks for this book and every. And my favorite saints (Dymphna, Anthony, Raphael, Michael, Gabriel Therese, Mother T., JPII, Max, Faustina, Rita, Monica, Gemma, the children of Fatima, Kateri, Philomena, and so many more), you know who they are!

So, you see, these are the people who make my life, my writing, and my world rich. Thank you to all!

"To improve is to change,
so to be perfect is to have changed often."

–Winston Churchill

A French Girl's Name

A French girl's name.
Jean Marie
A waste bucket full of red flowers
To my love a gift for thee.
Behind a mask I will
present them.
To hide my true identity
A French girl's name.

—Dr. Josephine A. Vitillo

Table of Contents

Royal Blue Shutters

Sonorous

Pressurized and rhythmic,
the night's buzz aped the howling
trees—irony mixed with superstition;
they wobbled in sapling form,
leafless sticks sown over the land—
birds and night owls
chanting with lynxes, a tie to every
living thing

Sounds staggered—hit nooks in trees;
a pleasant fusion of purple-blues
popped in the sky—
masks for the soul if anyone cared;
the periodic boom of fireworks
shifted feathered wings
(and windy groans) to specks of color
leaking through the blue-gray

Exhume

Bittersweet crossroads,
bizarre exercise in futility,
memories juggling—
too swift to be of any use
and far too complicated to decipher;
it makes her wonder if life's stacked
against her, two-tiered, retaliatory
She immerses her hands in the soil,
dirt so raw it smells like earth's husk
has finally peeled back, imparting its
                fleshy jumble of indecision;
there's no means of containing the salty
essence of bliss or terror's vague shadow,
a sort of welcome if she wanted to take it
that way, but somehow she understood her
presence here was part of a larger plan, a
way to establish a rhythm, wisdom's cycle

Split Luminosity

Jazzier than solar splendor—
fractured light—toggling between
a glimmer and well-lit gloss, such
a subtle system of nuances,
crystalline Morse code, riveting
flashes that required decryption;
not unlike the hushed murmur
of willows or the savvy smack
of a river's flow on shoreline rocks,
craggy, wetted, having their own
slick polish and split-second allure—

Charismatic as ever, light
endeavored to blend in, scintillatingly
lovely, shy, and curious, known to
make a spectacle often enough;
infused with transparency—one
miniscule, graceful breach
in a golden soul

Flux

Spinning her body in a circle,
arms outstretched, a row of storefronts
             twirling, pedestrian
walkways gyrating,
the shapes of men and women blurred—
one pirouette after another—either she
was performing them or the world was,
she hadn't the foggiest notion
until she stopped and fell to the ground,
the cold temperatures making her laughter
sound harsh; what a rush
             to dance in the streets,
something she rarely did anymore, those
years of dance academy untapped;
how she'd gotten the courage today
was a mystery; it could've been
             the chocolate croissant
for breakfast or her grandmother's pashmina
around her shoulders; either way, it felt good
to experience a world in motion

Mad for Jane

Her pulse quickened exactly
the same way every time she saw
him, and if she kept a diary she might
write about that beat-thump-beat

Or maybe she would forget
about writing and throw him down
on the bed to experience the weight of
his muscles pinning her against
the covers like a leaf pressed into a book

She had no guarantee he wouldn't
leave soon after they'd entwined,
though she shrank from the idea that he
loved her more each day

That night they sprawled by a fire,
orange flames foxtrotting through the logs,
vivid red wine on their lips, a brilliant
blaze which made her consider his
chiseled features and dark, tousled hair

Each berry he plucked from a bowl
dropped into her mouth, his fingertips
lingering there on her wet lips
as if he could never get enough of Jane

Shangri-La

Ulcerated and enraged,
the chafe and irk of losing his ticket
to paradise left him marooned,
his existence waterlogged, vision hazy,
swim trunks showing a line of white
rump flesh

Things rarely went his way
which kept him suspicious, fuming,
ready to point a finger, only he didn't
know who to blame or how to repair
the damage; that ticket meant a lot to
him—departure from a plastic job with
a pseudo-boss fond of cartoon neckties,
his game-show-host grin too artful

Perhaps it was his fault for
not locking the ticket in his bureau
instead of a quick shove in his breast-
pocket, an ill-suited place for something
so valuable, as if anyone could put a price
on his future, an oversight that might cost
him dearly for a long time to come

Leading Up to the Storm

Pinkish, the sky wore harlot's rouge,
billowy clouds flaunting their mass
like bosomy fishwives, the whole lot
of the heavens drunken and disorderly

Belching clouds jerked one way
across an attractive mauve sky,
perilously close to one another—a mating
ritual exposed to view; perhaps the next
morning their memories would fade,
but now the jolt of weightless clouds
matched the wandering eye of delicate
pink strands afloat on a blue background

An extravagant display of lust—
one so perfectly timed by the heavens
that the yip and growl of a thunderstorm
followed, its sharp call snapping against
the clouds, whip-like, the only sound
escaping from them one of pleasure

Royal Blue Shutters

The twist and turn of luck,
       the glow and blink of good
fortune—gold mine of elation; the
benefit of experience, know-how,
              ingrained optimism
and why some prospered while others
slid into doom's tipping egg basket—
the salty mystery remained; whether
Grant and Lila's outlook
would change, no one could say, but
after they'd won their fair share of the
pie, a bigger home with dormers and
royal blue shutters,
Lila blinked back tears

Curtains with lace trim
hung in the kitchen, a gray cat who
answered to Sugar licked his paws
on the sill

A storm flogged the upper basin,
a handful of days later—
beat the land unconscious,
shutters lying on the ground,
split in half—
Sugar refused to go outside;
neighbors boarded up their places
well into the night

Proviso

Generosity had a way of branching
out, an ability to grip impractical
things until they sprouted

Of course kind souls had green
thumbs; those garden terraces in
New York City were their doing

Every gala had its perks and the
ladies in tea gloves meant to hire
the best, refurbish the ghetto

If it were possible to paint the
entire thing Tiffany blue or
robin's nest teal, all the better

Six or seven committee members
stomped through the streets to
assess the project's scope

Yes, they needed more money
and fewer delays; one woman
broke her heel in a pothole

Oddly enough, generosity began
to twist, which meant it was limber,
able to reconfigure itself on cue

A Night with Elsa

Elsa's carte-blanche philosophy
toward men suggested she sampled
them regularly, those creative-types
with the wild eyes—men who didn't
understand her fully, the ones who
asked questions about her life

Leaking the truth about a spoiled
past might lead to random actions
on her part, if inclined to act at all,
but she'd sworn off any value in
being candid, so now it was simpler

Her cold-fish-mood flashed just as
the tall gentleman with the ugly feet
shared her warm body over bargain
wine and faint jazz; she gestured for
him to use the fire-escape soon after

Honest answers seemed too cozy,
and perhaps she was ill-fitted to a
life of wanting less but taking more,
a revelation that she would triumph
by never looking back

Dixie's Midnight

Shadows of the perfect gray
spread out over the compact, moss-grown
landscape; patios adjoined one another
in close city-living

Night's mild air fit like a coat,
snug in the shoulders, unbuttoned,
vivifying; each shadow played a role
in the spilled drinks of a guest or two;
as the grayness snuck up,
elbows jerked, cocktails jostled

Get-togethers with friends
on the patio—Dixie's way of loosening
up the pack for her stories in the
                    established midnight air

Whenever she rose above her five-drink limit,
she told the old favorites; the gang
listened partially—lukewarm air hit
their cheeks broadly
while the shadows twisted through the moss

Affection 2.0

Love's twin whispers reverberated,
the ping of happiness,
                    mushy-brained bliss;
it wasn't surprising to uncover how
the two traded in their single selves
to become a composite of each other,
ideas flowing from the same vat,
uniqueness relinquished for cozy,
                    neither one shuffled
their schedules that day, thinking
the other would be more willing, but
in the end the camping trip was off,
their love roasting over an open fire

He twisted his stick,
cool euphoria running through his
veins at a slower rate now; it was his
job to pack up all the gear, abandon
their plans to hike and canoodle
for no other reason than she couldn't
stand the sight of him anymore

In a frenzy, he stuffed
the car, pushed her knapsack roughly
inside, let the cookware clang against
the fender or be left behind

No ugly words on the drive home,
neither of them had anything to say

Undercut

The room throbbed with electricity,
hanging blue lights flickered, people's
voices raised, shrill, metallic—
not a damn thing she could do about it;
every town had its tiffs: if she'd stood
up sooner, imposed her viewpoint,
things may not have gone so far

Now she had to think the matter
through, redefine her role, bare her teeth
to the big corporation about to encroach;
the villagers' grip on the town had worked
itself loose, and the pit of her stomach
showed signs of warping—woozy, gnarled

Excavation of the site took months;
piles of dirt blocked her view, which
only made her roll up her sleeves; she owed
the quaint hamlet something for having left
all those years ago, thinking it too small
and slow for her, a nowhere-bridge

Briskly her vision cleared as the hole
in her town grew larger, childhood
memories scooped onto dirt mounds and
hauled away in trucks, portions of the
boondocks dissolving; she ought to fight
harder to save it—lay her body down—
a final chance to unchain her soul

Yielding

Pretty little dewdrop, hardly
identifiable in dawn's pastel glow,
morning's nip still grabbing the air—
a dot on a blade of grass

Vulnerable to the sun,
it expired with one ray's strike—
single dewdrop nullified by heat,
zapped into extinction

A sultry mess—earth's bitter plan
to let the sun rule, circular
yellow gadget for year-round warmth,
overlyglossy patina, the moon's
consequence

So starkly beautiful was the sun;
odds were the dew endorsed its own
sacrifice as green grass deferred to
noontime, bending gleefully

Quixotic Odyssey

A heel-turn brought him to the path's mouth,
slender spot with mud pools on either side,
a day of traipsing
through pale green muck
and dangling vines, the weight of the journey
thorny and pressing

Ruthless, soul-stabbing,
he might've turned back a thousand times,
no real reason for trekking—
ideas unscrewing in his head, as if
he'd brushed off the possibility
of surviving an uneven foot-stomp through woods

Due south, compass in hand,
the magnet spun—fists clenched
around a pack heavier than a mule, blacker
than any torment, miles ahead
appearing endless, fuzzy; he ought to consult
the wind's fresh slap on his forehead

He edged toward a groove,
finger-width little ditch with ants,
leaves, rainwater—his tongue dipped, watery
grit slid down his throat; it amazed him—
nature was at once enemy and friend,
untrustworthy, acquiescing—raw-muscled brute

Archway to the Farm

Red-lipped adversaries
thrived on details—thorny matters
no one else bothered with—
fixed scowls on their faces,
mirthful when gnawing on a bone

Beneath the archway, the taller
of the two men stood up and cleared
his throat, raising a set of keys
in the air, which jangled

Quaint countryside peeked
through the windshield as the men
hashed out plans for a merger, driving
through greenery on a dirt path,
farms and barns splayed out on hills

A wonderfully bumpy road
became a small comfort as they neared
Cuthbert's cabin—and if a series of
handshakes could boil a farm's blood,
a deal like this one just might do it

Ivan and Tara

Tenderness in mammoth
amounts
       dragged out the ceremony;
the couple kissed, hearty love-lock

What a surrender to value
their love so much, but confessions
were few—neither one betrayed
an instinct to run

Mid-June and mild,
trees swayed to summer songs
while Ivan and Tara cuddled fondly,
secure in the way they made
each other feel

Not abysmal to think
       of what could have been
       if the vows were put back
into their mouths, eaten, and swallowed,
soul-morsels, salty-tasting,
the kind Tara found humbling

Ivan preferred to nibble, naturally,
with teeth and tongue,
accepting his decision with one hand
on her breast

Secrets of the Moor

Mysterious,
       the drift of the night sky
          along the moor, a canvas
to be painted if bravery of that sort existed,
       her footprints solid on the peat;
          once the fog expanded, only
glimpses of her skirt's billowing hem
       appeared, each step slow and careful,
          the air's nip fierce; steadily she
crossed the surface, an outline of her figure
       traipsing over marshy ground, a heavy
          feeling in her chest, brick
companion, choked by dense air that was thoroughly
       unmistakable—glum nighttime's visage—
          she wanted to scream, but her voice
volumed-down, so she passed silently through
       the heath, sodden earth underfoot, clutching
          a tapestry handbag; perhaps she'd
roved too far—close-knit fog sagging all around her,
       no time to plan an escape; she was partly
          to blame—shy mistress from a rich
homestead channeling her energies on the moor,
       as if the drenched earth would welcome
          the balm of youth

Charlotte's Idée Fixe

The junk cluttering the sky
didn't seem real, white pianos
with their legs tucked under
to form clouds, a dizzying effect
as they spun counterclockwise

Eventually the keys loosened
and floated down, breaking apart
on the pavement; Charlotte jerked
her bag onto her shoulder and shoved
a handful past the zipper, each clanked
inside, her collection nearly complete

Endless hours of cloth-rubbing
revealed their gleam; it reminded her
of last week's hubcaps, the ones she'd
shimmied under the junkyard fence for,
tossing a dozen into the clearing; those
hadn't fallen from the sky, though

Amassing artifacts from the heavens
was her reason for stashing an empty
sack in her bike basket and never leaving
home without her pink-rimmed glasses;
she needed both to do this kind of work

The space under her bed was limited,
but surely she could squeeze the keys
next to the gray rubber elephant legs

Ark Of Cross Purposes

Problem's muck had cornered
a well-rounded man, some disputable

point (hardship's thickened wall), but
he'd decided to firm up his skills

and move on, granting himself
permission to build a boat as Noah

had done; collecting the two by twos
of every species, a taxing affair,

especially since a jungle beast had
almost clawed out his eyes, the number

of scratches upon his body multiplying;
indeed, his parched throat was a symbol,

devotion to the cause, hazy lines blurring;
he had no more energy to summon

the giraffes (affable giants), yet soaking
and heating more timbers until they'd

bend made his head spin . . . but the ark
wasn't done . . . it'd attract attention from

his competitors, crafty men who'd set out
after him, tamping down jungle weeds

with spears to copy his idea, dragging
snakes and goats into vans parked at the

edge of the path; it was amazing he hadn't
seen it before—their drive to outdo him,

a redundancy of arks—oh, he'd look like a
fool when they saw his tiger-pawed face

and wounded hands working wood over a
fire, its heat making his eyelids quiver, but

the time to give up had passed; he must
finish in order to secure the animals inside

and then wait for the storm (hours, maybe
days); perhaps a rest on his cot of vines

might relieve his spinning head; surely, he'd
earned the right to close his eyes until dawn

Turn Left at the Barn

In favor of hitching a ride
with some cowboy on the backroads—
hopefully one who'd left his hat on
but his horse behind—Melinda
smiled brightly and popped her hip out,
as if they'd know what it meant

Trucks stopped
one after another; only she preferred the
look of a cowboy in the driver's seat
and planned to sit tight until one arrived;
he'd take her where she wanted to go

Not much of a request
when she really thought about it—
her mama's place, where she hadn't
been since she was goat-small and
scared of grasshoppers for being green

She didn't know what to make of the
firm-jawed buck with the lazy smile
who eventually stopped,
hat tipped back as he scooped up her
bag, tossed it in back, told her to buckle
up—she didn't dare smile back, not for
the first thirty miles or so

No sense in seeming too eager to get
to Mama's place after all these years

Connoisseur

At block's end
a fantastic bistro
          doled out panini
more delicious than she'd ever tasted;
the savory flavor made her want to cry
just like every food critic
               in the five boroughs
So she tried to find fault with the grill
lines or garnish, the number of ham
slices piled high, pale cheeses melted
perfectly
                She would win
this battle with herself; watering down
her reputation with sparkling reviews,
too disastrous a move in a city with
legions of chefs
Maybe it was time to retire,
toss shrimp with scallions as she used
to do in her apartment
             overlooking Central Park

Fresno

Bewildered by a five-o-clock
        shadow that appeared by noon,
fairly mystified to possess
        an uncommon middle name, Wexley,
too fond of golf to forgo three
        weekends a month, duly unnerved
when Warren from the mail room
        parked in his executive spot—
Alexander roughly removed his navy blue
        tie and leaned back in his chair;
everyone had gone home, which
        meant he was free to think of Celia,
his lawyer-girlfriend who'd flown
        to Fresno, solo, her plans unclear,
his mind numb; perhaps he'd put too much
        stock in their relationship—
had he known she was about to dematerialize
        from his apartment, bed, life,
he would've mentioned how beautiful that
        snug red dress looked on her
when they'd gone to see *La Bohème* or how
        the sun was a notch under her hair's
amber hue, but it seemed too late for overtures
        now; he'd been foolish to lose her,
preoccupied with business and bottom lines;
        a West-Coast city had gained
the woman he loved, and he had to live with it

Daughter of the Winged Horse

The jump of her wings seared the sky;
Smoke echoed from the belly of a torn cloud,
lying on its side now, ripped open, a widening
gash, other clouds bumping into it, confusion,
eruption; a long neigh escaped her mouth,
daughter of Pegasus, an onus of expectation

What a delirious moment when she realized
Romulus' remarks had triggered her actions,
the vexing opinions of a non-Greek;
rich, loud laughter incited her to swoop among
the downy clouds, the trail of her golden mane
glorious—

Romulus must learn to stifle his judgments
before the tip of her wing found its way into
his belly too, a tragedy for which she'd shed
no tears, barbarous Romans, suckled
by a she-wolf, one brother slaying the other

Alluria contemplated the tales from high
in the sky, swooping lower to glimpse he who'd
called her lesser than Aura, her wings producing
gentle breezes with each flap

To end this strife, she must prepare the sky,
bring the heavens into agreement with her plan
to deliver a man on her back to a position beside
his brother, a challenge she accepted with zeal

Crusade

Brave deeds, the frills of a dauntless,
gritty hero whose essential nature it
was to surpass the heights of unease,
enmeshed in the silence of thinking
the matter through—no tactics poorer
than a martyr retracing his steps to the
tomb, unnerved, in search of greater
strength; a champion to uphold valor,
willing to cliff climb for mankind, one
edgy hero with blood on his sleeve, an
ego reinforced by fists ready to punch,
elemental, fierce, the only way to slay
his pride would be to reduce turmoil,
leave him with nothing but cheer and
wonderment; satisfaction transferred
its mirror image to fighting for justice,
though the hero shouted from the hill-
tops, deciding never to withdraw from
the clash, his concentration riveted on
the greater good—ever so timeworn.

Urbanite

The prickles in a tight-fitting
coat expanded her theory on
annoyances of the twenty-first
century to which she would
add hot dog relish on her shoe.
It took two blocks of zig-
zagging through a thick crowd
to reach the lime green door
of her apartment, a color choice
she'd never regretted. If one
couldn't wow an entrance, then
all was lost. She had several
possibilities for the afternoon,
including a singalong with her
cat, a feisty creature who hid
from her, spitefully. The good
news was she'd secured that
raise at work; her new office
would be walled, windowed,
and have a view. Of course
being an analyst had its down-
sides, but so did owning a cat
who didn't seem to care for
her taste in men.

Peripherally

Bend in the road,
not so straightforward as some,
utterly seductive as the curve of
a woman's hip—it reminded him of
wanton pleasures; he pressed the pedal
and sped forward, a convertible with
its top down; each windy blast hit his
face—he loosened his tie and let
the forceful gusts
spin it around his neck; no reason to slow
down since danger elated him, made up
for his slow childhood and two divorces
that dragged on; it was a pity he couldn't
extend his range—fly over the gorge,
land on the other side with his head intact,
truly he wanted to try,
but the edges of his vision hung back from
the drop, so he continued to shoot forward
in loops around the bend

Acquiring Sheep

Storms entered his life,
flecks of gold almost, how they
hung in the air before his eyes,
prisms of disaster, shiny, untouchable;
logically, he wanted to scream,

but a tantrum fanned out the flecks—
they clung to his torso, a suit of gold,
false armor—he felt squeezed

The purpose behind all of it was
greed, a desire for wealth, the happy
occurrence of grand fortune; he needed
money to start a business—raising pigs,
shearing sheep—wool and pork were
why the market boomed and profits
soared, he felt sure of it

Nevertheless, the men who grabbed
his hand and shook it firmly
controlled each fleck's direction,
something he hadn't counted on

It was going to be more difficult than
he'd thought to acquire sheep

Drifting Banter

Stray voices lingered in the air,
pebbly, distinctive,
a stunning brogue; many ignored
the wisps of conversation, dispersing
down boulevards
and up one-way streets; their voices
failed to go with them,
a counterblow, salacious air
caressing an articulation that was
not its own; silver-haired
gossips overheard morsels of odd
remarks as the workforce
headed to industry jobs with lunch
sacks and stone-chiseled
gazes, hardened by effort and worry

Nighthawk

Those screechy, beautiful sounds
and that navy quirky sky
demanded her attention; perhaps
the birds' darkened bodies
collapsed in flight, but the sky
showed no signs of catastrophe other
than its heavy-handed push of
gauzy clouds further north;
highly amusing, she thought, to have
a world where birds
inferred the sky's temperament;
awkwardly, she craned her neck,
gawking at a night hawk—
its eyes flashed like blinking marbles,
seemingly aware of every
movement—a knowledgeable pilot
with a dinner plate on the moon;
oh she knew the hawk's
territory reached less far, but any
swoop and glide was a
mission she understood, one she
had intentions of admiring

Woodland Prowl

Tidy windfall fed a junket
out west to glorify
giant spans of redwoods—
numerous woodsy hikes flattened
her back for uphill climbs,
magnificent terra-cotta bark
clothed trunk after trunk,
a dizzying effect; she thought
nothing of tilting her head to spy
the forest's bulk, attracted
by a formal symmetry,
dragged further into its hum-beat,
a strip of water bending
the soil snakelike, narrow, twisting
unlike northern creeks
with their cheery meandering;
she surmised the utility
of exploring the leafy outgrowth
casually as her heels
skipped through the thicket of the bosk

Agog Wooers

Bright and durable—a brunette
with wide hips—capable of mollifying
two suitors and their doltish jokes
with a deep laugh;
wildly flashy smile, premature
and fitful,
oozed cool charm,
stemming off casualties, if ever these
two half-brothers should meet;
their adoration for her had ripened,
a twice-over love—
miniscule hope that she would
marry either one; their chests narrowed
to lean waists, small tufts of
centered hair; it appealed to her,
moderately,
men with brooding souls,
if she could imagine
building a life with such a man
or his brother

Johnny and the Saltwater Tide

Puckered up to a pre-lit sun
melting on an ultramarine horizon,
the ocean's brassy tide surrendered
its erotic oomph;
ladies' legs dangled
in olive-drab waves
while hairy-chested men wandered
over to chat with them—

Romantic fool with a steady gaze,
passion's soft spot
shook and sputtered, dawdling
to the far edge of lust and back;
a bottle of wine swung forward
from its hidden position
behind a man's back, eyes squinty
with an idiotic smile

Pink-toed ladies sipped
from the bottle, eyeing Johnny
as he jabbered about fish and how
to catch the big one;
rougher now, the tide splashed under
the dock—nighttime's coral-blush

Tawny Satchel

Pleased to announce her ability
to step up in a complicated world, she
lugged a bulging satchel, rosy apples
curved against buff leather,
the sum total of her life defined by the
distance a lonely red sphere
traveled toward the sky—as it crept
into the air, hurled delicately
from her fingers, she wondered about
life's little complexities
and how a baker of apple pies fit into
a bigger plan; goods at the outdoor
market brought hungry crowds, folks
who sorted apples by color,
preferred spoons for pie-eating; she'd
baked hybrids this time—
peach-kiwi-apple, a farmhand favorite,
and raspberry-apple-nut;
new flavors with old recipes turned
out unexpectedly well, which
got her thinking on the tawny satchel—
if she should carry it any longer

Ava's Quandary

Tied to logic
and methods of understanding,
hasty decisions unsettled her—
cut off oxygen to her brain,
wholeheartedly twisting a stellar
intellect's framework;
rather quickly,
a pile of considerations emerged,
ones she wished
neither to brush off nor to ponder

Outthinking the opponent—
what she considered to be
the widest point of any obstacle—
took expert fixity;
going off on a tangent served no
purpose, precisely why
she never indulged in fruitless
efforts; for now, she must
unwrap the problem delicately

Hindsight

Roomy naïveté—
breadth and width to be naïve—
he imagined how life would be
had he made different choices,
culled an untwisted path

Curiously unmerciful, the tide
washed away his marks in the sand—
his past never really vanished;
one glance over his shoulder drew
him back in bold reverse

Weak-legged, he jogged
up the beach in a direction he'd
considered too bumpy initially,
spotting seagulls swiftly carrying
shells into the air

He'd gotten it all wrong—
narrow-nosed fish darted and swam
deeply along a blurry bottom;
segments of a sea-green edge
eroded informally as he looked on

Weak waves grazed his kneecaps,
a tangle of faults, sand-grit
clinging to his legs, thighs,
and buttocks; an immovable beach,
no way to retrace his steps

Toward the Fire

The shouts and shudders
of daylight had him reaching
for the frayed, woolen edge of an
army-green blanket to pull over
his eyes. Camping was the
easiest thing in the world until
sunshine cracked brightly
and his head spun
on a pole; at least it seemed
that way. Too many beers by the
campfire last night had him
roughly morose this morning,
not to mention his buddies out
on the lake fishing in the quietude

He envisioned eggs and bacon,
but the fire had died out;
cavernous growls from his belly
provoked him; only something
poked into his back through the sleeping
bag—stick, rock, tree root—
he wiggled onto his knees, then
stumbled toward the fire

Golden Agers

Tiny little diamonds splashed
on a band, a shaky pair
of hands steadied the ring;
white-dove reluctance on a wedding
day; fresh whisper, darling jasmine
posy, softly esteemed, the couples'
faces sagged—splendorous,
hammock-like; two eighty-year-olds
beaming in tux and gown—
the fragrance of youth conforming
to a wine glass, red-tinted, stupendous,
half the size of their love

Guests in hair ribbons smiled stiffly,
hands clasped in their laps;
the strum of a guitar trotted the bride
down the aisle, footsteps on a lane
of grass, flowery trellis where a priest
stood, righteously thick Bible
squarely on a podium—true love's
push about to take hold

Jaded

Retreat on the northern side
of the shore
vaguely resembling a butterfly—
crouching, resisting, trying to
look meaningful,
a dalliance if she were to guess,
opposed to the flit of Tiffany wings,
beauty's spectacle

a waste of her precious
time, an injudicious approach to
an afternoon walk
                        beyond the pier

Surely it was the mountainside
that brought its weight down on
the minds of anyone near it,
not the wispy-winged butterfly,
a piece of chiffon in the wind—

perhaps she should thank the alp
for its civil objection
to small creatures close at hand,
the privilege to impress its peaks
was not theirs,

and it struck her as frivolous—
a butterfly's fragility against
the cloudless sky

Rowing Out

Sizzling lightning on the waves—
the glare off the water—bright white outline
that crested and crashed; how far had they rowed?
A column of ripples battered their paddles, not
a day for river-mastery; the selected current forced
them to pivot and spin,

a binding agreement with water's unending roll—
slightly inefficient, unfit to stay dry, neon-yellow
shirts stuck to their bodies while a good-natured
grip on the oar slipped

Goose necks would've been easier to grasp,
and growing up on a farm they were, yet
there wasn't time to ponder it; tall waves
climbed and sheets of water tumbled down

on men rowing against a monster, the beast
of the sea, this river's jealous rage—
to strain their muscles, to consecrate them
as weak; listless bodies if they dropped
their guard—a single moment for the struggle
                                      to leave them

Wind pushed aside their voices, but the one
with plank-width shoulders hollered to the other,
sunshine warming their foreheads,
fear nestled in their eyes; he would be the one
to save them, if only he could catch his breath

Three Instruments

In all honesty she had no intention
of speaking her mind in the middle
of a concert

Ironically the woodwind section
sounded sharp *and* flat,
fluent in a banned language

Perhaps fresh air would rouse her
or cool water from the lobby—
dingy fountain near a display case,

gold trophies lined up,
but her thoughts reverted to the man
with a finger to his lips, glasses

halfway down his nose, polka-dot
tie to match his unappealing smile;
he'd given her a stern look when

she'd sneezed in a series,
condemnation in the slant of his eye-
brows; the decision to scamper toward

the back and through the doors
calmed her nose, though it may have
been the distance from his tweed

jacket that relieved her; chilly sips
of water formed a dewy path down
her throat; she stopped short

of splashing any on her face;
the finale came next with solos by
clarinet, flute, oboe; she rushed

to her seat only to find him gone;
the man with the pointy nose had
left, allowing her to listen freely

Separate

Few understood her desire
to be alone,
a book with no pages,
a sweater unraveling,
the teacup empty;
rarely did it disturb her
to know they pitied
the person she'd become

Privately, she knew
the soft voice of solitude
worked in strange ways—
it talked her into daring
things: skydiving and
dying her hair maroon;
of course she fancied the
repartee, which, at times,
seemed chatty, as if
quietude longed to draw
her out, unwilling
to define the contessa
until she defined herself

Jalopy

He tinkered with the engine;
a few puffs of smoke told him
he might be getting somewhere

Cobwebbed Chevy in the barn
needed a solid month of repairs,
but he only had the weekends

Squiggly scar on his wrist
reminded him of last month's
attempt to fix the rocker panels

He'd been careless—the damn
thing still hurt; good reason to
blame his ex-wife for that, too

Past few months he'd been
picnicking with a blond school
teacher, half a dozen dates

Could be he'd found the one—
but getting his hopes up wasn't
his style; he'd wait and see

Lure, Resist, Gratify

Brash, boorish wind left her hair
undone at the nape, an unplanned
mishap; she pivoted, pinning
it in place—took pains to anchor
each strand soundly. For Raul, she
must appear angelic, sent from
above with a nymph's heady smile

What good would it do to sour an
au fait lover of her fairness?
She ought to maintain glamor's
bloom for the raw, wintry
eyes of the man who probed hers
in the dark

Passion buzzed in his brain,
erotic whoosh, airy, primal kisses
diffused on her collarbone,
such easy charm to carve sensations
along those soft, fleshy tips
of feminine earlobes; he howled to
please her; the young night
growing risky, the more he shifted
against Mara's silky neck

Wedding Path

Awash in pageantry, a tree-lined
lane led to a footbridge—a pair of lovers
traversed it neatly, hand-holding,

the sky's blush dotting her cheeks
as the wind's curlicue forced a lock of his
hair to tremble above one eye;

not as magnificent as yellow-orange
tones skimming the topiaries, to the naked
eye an overly sophisticated sunset;

on a puff of breath, she whispered the
bridge's history—how townsmen had nailed
the planks by hand, then branded

their initials with the fiery tip of an
iron poker; kneeling, she ran her fingertips
over the darkened grooves, awed by

the past and her upcoming betrothal,
the man beside her encompassing her dreams,
the days to the ceremony fewer and fewer

Deep Roots

Disappearing beneath the trim
of her black lace veil
gave her peace

as if the circumstances were
slowly sinking in, now
that she'd cried

Obviously, the man who'd built
his life in tandem with
hers was gone

There was nothing left to do but
reenter daily existence
with more clarity

Only she had qualms about being
lonely, regretted buying
groceries for one

The idea of knitting a scarf, doing
yoga, climbing mountains
didn't interest her

Time would be lengthy now, since
the man she loved was no
longer by her side

Madhouse

Once rapture eroded,
the state of love mildewed

lust rotted out, too—a merry
band —only bliss snapped

in half unevenly, its larger portion
irregularly shaped; quite frankly, no

one could tell them apart, which led
to scuffles and quarrels, ones that left

bliss to hyperventilate and lust to lie
on the bed all day; love tried every-

thing to remedy the situation—softly
spoken words, candlelight dinners for

four, but rapture's mood swings
were impossible to overcome, so love

devised a plan—sent out invitations
cluttered with hearts and kisses on the

envelopes—a party thrown by rapture,
love, lust, and bliss; of course cupid's

second cousin took one look at it and
threw it in the trash, refusing to go

Chloe of the Woods

The entrance was narrow,
threadlike; she contorted to pass
through—barky sides scraped
her hips and elbows
as she hunkered down,
a wombed being, perhaps
put off by her own plan
to scrutinize hardwoods

She'd spent hours sifting
through bramble, observing
water tables, carrying out her
duties to assist nature
in the only way she knew how,
scientifically,
a collection-sample kit tied
to her belt, a flimsy net sheltering
her face from bugs, but she paused
frequently

Her evaluation of nature—
the creek's erratic flow, thicket's
tender chant, a tree's purr—
was intimate, well-matched,
a union she'd sanctioned

Ocean's Chant

Devoted to the bleakness
of the morning—
that spiffy angular beast—
ocean waves rolled as she swept
back her hair, unable to view
vibrant-rich swells
as the gait of her own thoughts
flitted

Only it revealed itself to her—
an ocean of unending relapses,
each zealous push
another birth of tangled seaweed
choked by shells
and fish—the roar of new life
yeasty beneath the surface

It yearned to churn her, too,
a fleck of froth upon its breast,
supine, doll-like creature
made to undulate unduly, quick
whip of her senses,
head bobbed, blue sky, peculiar
modulation of voice

Swell after swell dripped
green-current's
slush; it was what she had
come to know

Mythology's Mirror

Lacking fiery beak:
dragon's wit to ridicule a bird's flight,
challenged and disturbed, a scaly beast
flapping gorge-width toward a nest,
humble eggs, a beautiful pattern
of airborne swirls to glide homebound,
only a ribbon of water below snaked
through rocks, giving the dragon pause,
as if drinking from the blue brook
asserted power and youth; semi-wonder
to dive toward its beryl basin,
an array of reflections darted to the sky

Not the type of intricate landing a beast
of this sort could perform—
abruptly its narrow nose dipped into
sweet-tasting water; all the birds flew off,
maddened, scurrying, scorched by fire
if the dragon wished to spew any, if set
upon by a flock of birds

Slope-Mount

Crags in a tilted wall of rock
curved and looped,
the combination of crevices
an archaic cursive, handwritten,
squiggly symbols requiring
scholarly interpretation, a jargon
she suspected had something to do
with the jagged slope,
a warning she disregarded blithely

Raw, instinctively, she coveted
the climb—seduction and lure of an
upward trek—tiny glimpses
of branches, leaves, greenery far below,
her foothold strong and steady,
a full breeze firmly at her back

Angular splay of stone—spiked,
unleveled—a high point where weeds
jutted through cracks,
pale flowers vaingloriously perched,
as if they'd summited
as she had, only with minimal effort

Affinity

Quick pleasure on an upswing of love,
tenderly unequivocal, forward-stepping
into nirvana's petal-soft hideaway—
posh bedroom of moans,
caresses, rumpled bedsheets,
        faint fragrance of snapdragons,
low howl of music drifting down
into the alley, deep shadows
tried by love's potent kiss; he smoothed
out her spine with his fingertip
        She eyed croquet balls
on the sill and a pot of cold tea near the
headboard, her British lover's
affinity for drink and sport: rising, she
ran her hand along his calf, a silent
request for him to meet her in the shower,
early morning light several hours off

Root Cellar

Black gulley storm popped
flower-heads off—
slant and thrust of rain propelled
muddy yellow dots on a slim,
haphazard tide,
river's bend down a mile;
darkened, petty equator divided
knotty pines from wind's snap
but only against the back forty's
upper portion; townsfolk
shook themselves out, if it'd
ever ease up

Middle America buckled—
nature pulsed
like the vein in a farmer's forehead—
grit spewed, big-fisted claws
reached out to flay and rend;
blobs in the sky
torpedoed the corn and melons;
thickened rain masses
descended by gravity's demand
while quick-thinking men guided
horses into barns—wives
and children into the root cellar

Carmelina

Overlapping birdsong had lodged
in her mind, familiar sounds
of delicately necked creatures with shrill
lyrics, the hum and cackle of sky-fliers;
the degree to which she'd gaped
as they'd split up in trees,
a hop along ever-thin branches—
simple dance to dignify beak-chatter.
She dared not rest her eyes
as they rhumbaed far above, yodeling
cleverly before diving lower; she swung
her neck to where the two
most colorful might land, distantly
in a sycamore, and heard their soft
communication—diluted gurgling—
which reminded her
of vodka trickling down a man's throat,
only a dull beauty
became the birds' calls; nothing a man
could achieve with a drink

Rider

Nonchalantly, she took hold
of the reins, as if the horse
would follow her direction,
but its mane swung and tickled
her chin—flirtatious animal—
she galloped onward
to her destination, one so shadowy
and treed she almost closed
her eyes, wept for what she must
do; claps of thunder pierced
the sky, a sloppy version of rain,
but oh, she had to carry the message
deeper into the woods

Stark Raving Mad

Not oblivious to the countless people
who stood there gawking as she
decreased in size
almost to a dot, except
her head refused to vanish

Luckily, she believed in herself
even if her soul appeared cockeyed—
it was not the true cause of her dishevelment

The reasons were painted on the wall
beneath which she wiggled on the fleshy
earth until a tall man ejected himself
from the crowd
and kneeled down beside her

In a voice softer than a rose pedal;
he asked simple questions;
only her head swam, mind buzzed
until the clouds in the sky were hazy,
rumpled cotton sheets
that she had no desire to separate

She was done with folding them,
done with excuses in general

Upended

Bodiless she seemed as her limbs
bent in all directions, a way to float
toward the sky,
though flapping her wings
would alert the others

She wanted nothing but the hush of
the cold earth against her back
and perhaps a sip of dew on her lips
to quench the stiffness of floating
up, up, up—

Inhaling the fragrance of the pines
and the permanent whiff of weeds
along the edge of her gown
she spanned her arms out
as far as they would go

It wasn't necessary to speak or hum
or hear the drift of the river's course,
that swift babble

No, she didn't care for any of that;
no, it was not what she was about

Momentary Bliss

Massive amounts of joy seeped
into her soul and knocked around
inside her like so many wooden
mallets,
threatening to
overwhelm the tiny space

The mock fury
she felt subsided when the joy did

But as the joy vanished and the
clamor in her depths
no longer banged and rustled,
she wondered if sadness
was more efficient

as it left her vacant
and quieted, unable to complain

Consequential Beauty

How meticulously the woman
arranged her hair, as if the bun
atop her head had set up camp

No one knew the pleasure she
got from wrapping the strands
and making them stay

But certainly the men in the
room would do their best to
shake her down

They wanted the bun to topple,
so they could grapple with her
and perhaps arrange a date

Only she saw their fury and
managed to press a hat over
the bun and stalk off

Hitchhike

Delicate wavelengths oscillated
in her mind as she craned her neck
out the window

What she hoped to see was anyone's
guess, but then it was just like her to
poke her head out and see the world
on its ear

Delicate mayhem she used to say and
sigh into the night

Long after she straightened her neck
and closed the window, the shadows
of every sort of tree creeped over the
roadway like gray ropes

It made sense to offer the man a tip—
his kindness in driving her out this way—
but she knew the night might swallow
them both

Ode to Adam

Ravaged apple trees reminded her
of Eve, the twinkle of sin that
slithered, oh the best apples, the
biggest, reddest, roundest were out
of reach

The woman's eyelids grew heavy,
a weight so pronounced she called
her husband to inform him—
How are we to eat? she moaned,
a cackle more than a cry

He shook his head, both hands
on his hips,
then ascended the ladder and plucked
the fruit, letting it plunge to the ground
at her feet

There, he said, go ahead and devour
what I've brought

Ode to Eve

She wove another braid in her
daughter's long hair, an inspiring
natural elegance that mimicked the
vines all around them

She stopped only to explain one thing
to the child—matters of life and death

Fear struck the child as her mother told
a tale so vile,
so wretched, that each piece of the
braid unwound, and as it did so,
the child spun in the air, faster

But her mother shrieked one word,
and the girl fell into her lap

Remember what I taught you, she said,
and redid the braid with violet ribbons,
green leaves, and amber twigs

From Her Diary

God didn't explain his reasons to me
about replanting that tree in the middle
of the garden, at the nexus of several
flowering bushes on either side, magnified
by glorious blooms, petals so interlocked

What an array of beautiful plants, each
clinging to the path; what lush holdovers
of what could have been—

Surely, Adam tells me not to blame
myself for the events of that first day

But before the thunder came and boomed,
prior to the shake of olive trees,
the coarse, grim rumble of stunned animals,
howls loud enough to split the earth in two—

I sensed I was being watched;
of my own accord I followed the woman
past the hills and into the desert,
drank when she drank,
slept when she slept

Behold

It was a gross display of clouds
banging against the walls of the earth
which told her how lonely the atmosphere
had become,
like a stepchild
only boxed into a corner
with pins and needles for friends

No delight could be found when
the elegant mist passed over the low valley,
and the calmness of the land smeared
the hilltops

Cloud masses pummeled the sternly
beautiful blueness
of the sky
like a dome of little old ladies holding
hands as they told war-time stories—

It was their downfall, rhythmic
to the end

The Singer

The purpose of the universe
dragged her thoughts in and
out of focus, like a cloth wiped
over a tabletop, a waitress
too thorough

Fishnet stockings, cherry-red lips,
she sang about the cosmos
at the nightclub
to an audience duller than wood
grain and drunker than whiskey

Not to give up her mission
to find answers—why, how, where
the stars fell and on whom—
with what kind of force

Jar full of dollar bills smashed
to the floor, useless tips;
she needed answers

Rooftop Balcony

Intersections between here and there,
not uncommon,
identifiable when properly
examined,
accountable to the single
eye
at
the
end
of
a
tele-
scope

But her night vision was off, or the
stars had gotten less bright—
she hoped they'd never fade
altogether

Zephyr

Far off the sky appeared
from her presence on the dune,
a wholly soggy stone's throw
from the bay's whipping wind
and algae patches

The decided gale tempted her—
bold holler twisting in the wind
as she dipped her toes
in the bay, shaking a fist in the air

Sandy dunes so soft and enviable,
biscuit-shaped lump of earth
sitting beneath the sky

At the Picnic

Decked out in jewels that sparkled
into the grass and over the rocks,
the sun glamorized the land for
as many hours as it could hold
position

No rains came, and not an ounce
of gloom doused the hot yellow day,
and every bright ray shot an arrow
into the field

Which left the pebbly dirt shiny
and the children running through it
with their laughter echoing,
and the adults moseyed in the grass,
their legs crossed and mouths open

Tremendous heat pressed the temples
of each one, hotter and more brilliant
than a summer's day

The Turf

Shocked and horrified, the girl
squirmed and finally stood, knees
covered in dirt and bullies all around
but never a broken spirit, fully agile

She called out to see if anyone might
appear to prevent the bloodshed

The turf was hers just as much as theirs,
and it was about time she blurred the lines
on their faces—prove she could fight—
curled fists at her sides

Headlong she ran like a button popping
off a coat; only her coat lay on the ground

. . . only her coat lay on the ground . . .

Long Forgotten

The thump of rain sounded like a yelp
to her, so she shifted and peered out
the windowpanes, but
the brutality of the downpour
sliced into the grass very quickly

She watched with fluttering eyelids
the straight slants of transparency;
of course the patter on the roof
was rhythmic, and it made her think
of playing the violin;
if only she hadn't promised to keep
it hidden, chained

Her thoughts weakened as the rain
beat down
but eventually her desire to make
music brimmed

She pounded on the cabinet door
until the wooden instrument released,
tucking it under her chin,
dragging the bow over strings

Progression

The tick of the clock failed to move
her life forward,
so she had to climb onto the wall
and adjust the hands

The very act of climbing
landed her foot on the filing
cabinet and her waist against the
calendar

She felt odd in that position,
but it had to be done
in order to move her life forward,
the very thing that could move it

seemed so unreal; she should have
asked for help, consulted someone first—
only there hadn't been time;
the day was already there

Intense Ardor

Oh, the ramifications of sniffing
      her perfume-scented neck
caught him by surprise;
how fond he'd grown of her heroic beauty,
      the muscle-jerk of love,
split-second release of velvety hormones
capsizing his willpower,
      a whiff of that neck, unbearable
beauty, round curving hips, thighs
and buttocks—he reached out—
to toss her aside, an excuse to maintain
      his right mind; her adorableness
sired sensations no man could bear,
      and he would put a stop to it—

He drove home under navy blue skies,
      owls hooting so loudly
it startled him—
      their awareness of his shame

Heuristic Exercises

The ridicule she felt for weaving
thoughts inside the milk bottle of life
only posed a greater dilemma—
the tedious rarity
of finding a solution to an age-old
dispute; not that she minded
calling the headmaster a lumberjack—
he was everything but—as long as
she could travel freely between
her mind and the baggy portal
                where all this seemed to occur,
the forefront of spiritual connection—
an instant of nothingness—people counted
on her to find out the truth
of course, she hoped to win this war prior
to life's conclusion,
              though she had to wonder

Lush Meadow

The ratio of love's
magnetic pull
to its all-encompassing warmth
lagged behind industry standards,
scientifically speaking,
and the couple
in the meadow kissed openly,
fervently—
starvation on love's diet,
lips and tongues,
fools caught up in the moment;
buttercups at their feet,
the rims of their eyeglasses
touching;
wind skipped through weeds,
bright yellow dandelions
dotted the hill. They'd both
left work early
to meet outside of the lab,
in the lush meadow

Crossing the Surface

The cravings she felt were for Earth's
belly to swallow her up,
a morsel at a time, eventually releasing
her soul into the air beyond the clouds—
a shimmer near the sun,
and yet her yearning to understand
had put the Earth off,
leaving her alone, holding a coffee cup

Everything seemed drained
of volume, light, wiggle-room; indeed,
she was tightly squeezed
against Earth's bosom—her hair pressed
into her neck and her nostrils
felt pinched; she yelled for help but then
jabbed a finger into Earth's eye-socket—
                    what a distinctive yelp,
one she'd never forget, even if someday
its secrets were proclaimed,
but bravery of this sort may not visit her
again unless she could prove herself
worthy

French Art Salon

The tapestries interchanged—
gurgled on the spot,
carpet dragons on walls,
hollow beings set to ignite,
                 boost the blaze,
surely they appeared bland,
statically dangling,
even insignificant to the vast few,
but a sense of wonderment defied her,
made her instantly alert
to her surroundings—the domed
building with notable artworks,
extraordinary gems,
art lovers mulling about; it tried her
patience in many ways—
                 solid-gray fusion
of understanding, the discharge of
volatile aspirations,
a minimization of her own creativity,
as if her work could only fall
short of these heights

tête-à-tête

                    In uneven strides,
they wended forward, their journey's sway
more of a polite stagger, edging
toward a bush whittled into pineapple form,
luscious yellow-green monstrosity
                         befuddling the park—
the top portion fanned out in fierce dominion,
an element of surprise if one wasn't aware
                      Vibrant delay in an
explosive reaction of lips
and roaming hands, each underwent a rapid
rush of breath, entwined
in lust's powder keg; the kiss beside the bush,
tender lover's moment;
neither made a move to undress—the park,
guarded by lanterns, preposterous beams
of light—they must proceed
cautiously, abide by the terms of their secrecy

Burrow Down

She sought the center of the universe
                    in drop-down patterns,
the darkest enviable resolution was clear
if only she'd take the leap,
                    but it presented a problem—
the indecisive melancholy of it all,
under-riding factors looming,
                    sheer panic to reach the core,
her faculties mesmerized
                    with regrets, frothy
misgivings on what she was about to do—
revealing the inner workings of the cosmos,
                    an utter disadvantage if she
failed to follow its rules and observe
the unique joy a discovery like this could mean;
                    to say it penetrated her soul
underwhelmed,
and hiking up her legs to overcome rocks
in her path only made her stumble more—
time would tell if she had the guts to
                    burrow down

Temporal Lag

Stolen moments of time shot out
                              spidery fingers
hijacked by a syncopated beat,
                    one that thumped repeatedly,
relentless tempo, unstoppable cadence, truly
something to knock the average person off
                              their complacent stoop;
a numb feeling flowered inside her, so grave
were the circumstances; she had hoped for
                                        better,
but now she knew her fate, what lay ahead—
developments that would only outcast her
from the drum beat, the one she could hear
                    when the rain splintered to
                              the ground,
and far better would it be for her to stop now
and put an end to stolen moments—only she
didn't want to scourge them with her whip,
quite ruthlessly,
nor designate herself commander
                              of this mission,
seeking to slow down time's apparent flight
in all directions—unable
                    to be snared or shoved—
a rampant form of hardcore journeying,
                    time's accustomed companion

Getaway, Malarkey Style

In twilight's twisted glow, an allegory
arose, tight, shadowy campfire
with yellow licks of light as high as
the sky from the lips of Saint Marcus—
one phenomenal storyteller—they referred
to him that way on the outskirts of the city,
a seedy place of slick clients, used cars,
and bad deals
                No one bothered to correct
the shady practices in case it diluted their
weekends of wilderness fun—a chance to
be away from wives, drink beer,
spit on the ground, share lies
                They cuddled beside
the fire, trapped by its light, pretending to be
fearful of the legacy of Santo Marcus
who told of his exploits
              in Parma and Napoli,
not caring to elaborate as the fire grew dim; it
was enough to know he'd done his part
for these drunken fools

Lie in Sunlight

Summer triggered its own fragrance,
scarlet-red blooms heated through;
a day in the sun made them fleshy,
entwined in jolly wind gusts

Wild morning glories hatched
in dirt-road ditches, random splashes
of periwinkle; an aroma of petunias
sifted in and out of spindly saplings

A farm with large hay bales
squatted on land regally, accented by
dandelions and whiffs of manure,
the grandiose measures of farm life

Sequential sunshine collapsed
on grassy plains, maximizing
crystal-clear gleams across yellow-
green fields that reached for miles

From Portland

The saddle hook of love
burnished the bridle of remorse
he felt for falsifying

his whereabouts to a debutante,
his dainty-waisted cousin from Portland
who'd arrived to spend a summer's

week in Colorado riding horses on
the land; only he'd flown to Tahiti
with a woman he'd met—and he knew

it was love by the way she sank her
teeth into his jaw when they rolled on
the bed—which left the poor girl

alone in his apartment with nothing to
do; she tipped her head back, dropping
take-out noodles into her mouth

wholly craving some fun away from
her parents; if only she could find a
gentleman to show her around; she

ought to try the café in town, a chance
to let her Oregon roots shine; maybe
twist her long blond hair up

Skin of the Sky

Thunderbolts stripped the sky
of its serene intentions, fraying clouds
and graying out scenery, thrusting
crickets from the grass

Hovering bees sipped silken
flowers while the storm's vibrations
twitched their wings, such a tense
deliverance from placid blue

A fury of raindrops smacked
the ground, more like mallets than
nourishment; each strike bounced
up from the dirt, rhythmically

Rumbling thunder jiggled among
blackened clouds, intense silver
lines—jagged alabaster—rods of
lightning against the skin of the sky

Dove-Like Breeze

Her genesis was of the blander
sort—a gentle breeze in a park
after which her parents laid
down in the grass; she knew the
story's unwavering details
but always wondered if her quiet
personality stemmed from
that breeze—and if they'd chosen
a different spot she might be
dauntless

Her authority to inquire
about the days prior to her birth
earned her soft smiles
from her mother who nodded for
more tea

Dove-like breezes had sparked
her into being, something she
had tried to wrap her mind around
before; only she knew
her mother had left something out,
a major detail

"Tell me again how you met
my father. What did he whisper
to you in the park?"

Shoddy Elixir

The jack-eyed look of a man
who'd sworn off booze
produced an authentic thud
in his temples—a pounding to uproot
every vein in his head—quite an
exhilarating shock
that he'd wasted all that time
on a bar stool

Ineloquently, he slid on a pair of
coveralls and grabbed
his tool belt; he'd fix something,
even if it killed him

Halfway between a ramshackle
barn and a pristine strawberry
patch, weeded by his wife,
religiously, he realized how foolish
he must look,
scratching the stubble on his chin,
plodding through tall grass
toward a rusty fence—
sun cracking down on his head

Yet hard work's charm swung
at his waist
in the form of a hammer, the fields
full of proof that a man
could return and be welcomed

Sleek Rain

A fresh beat of rain
rotated mist through pine trees,
the wet shoulder of love never
cried upon; an irreverent and tyrannical
haze settled in the clouds, sprayed
down nickels and dimes as clear as
glass, but sodden. Milky dew may have
shone if the sun flashed,
but it didn't dare yellow the drips
along curved branches—
the dull gray sky leaked envy
and rain's flask emptied—
dank, wettish steam rose across
a flattened valley, trees parted on either
side, whitish ghosts hovering
as miniscule amounts of gooey warmth
floated upward; rain's glow soaked
the ground—to dry up eventually,
                  firmer earth to unfold

Third Date

The trip wire of love satisfied
his desire for dim candle dinners
with a woman whose jewelry flashed
in the low light

Although her eyes failed to sparkle,
the honey-rich luster of her soul made
up for it; a thick, ripe laugh stabbed
his ears from her bright pink lips

An armful of bracelets glided
to her elbow as she ran a finger along
her jawline, studying him like an
artifact in her collection

With a wave, he ordered more wine
and shared a joke he'd overheard
on the subway; legs crossed, she stifled
a laugh and twirled a fork through greens

By dessert, he'd reached across
the table to cover her hand with his;
she blinked and spoke of an antique shop
in the heart of the city

He focused on her pink mouth
that curled up at the edges, sublimely;
no doubt she'd have a million ways

Fragmentation

A trash heap of memories—
broken backlash of thought—
widespread inconsistencies in how
life plays out—
mesmerizing swirl of blunders,
soul-creeping and dark,
not unlike the deep grunts
of rusty songs
people mutter on subways—
purely guttural hum of voices,
blurred epitome of white picket
fences, oh the lag of
knowledge that fails to bristle
when bright things sink
away from us

Previously Published

"From Her Diary" *The Emerson Review*, Vol. 47, April 2018

"Sonorous" *The Ibis Head Review*, Vol. III: Issue 2,
        June, 2018

"Shangri-La" *The Ibis Head Review*, Vol. III: Issue 2,
        June, 2018

"Split Luminosity" *3Elements Literary Review*, Issue 19,
        July 2018

"Ava's Quandary" *The Blotter Magazine*, July 2018

"Tawny Satchel" *The Blotter Magazine*, July 2018

"Urbanite" *The Blotter Magazine*, July 2018

"Ivan and Tara" *Adanna Literary Journal*, Issue # 8,
        August 2018

"Flux" *Adanna Literary Journal*, Issue # 8, August 2018

"Mythology's Mirror" Classical Mythology Edition of
        Curating Alexandria, June 2019

"Crusade" Classical Mythology Edition of *Curating
        Alexandria*, June 2019

"Daughter of the Winged Horse" Classical Mythology
        Edition of *Curating Alexandria*, June 2019

"Progression" Atlas and Alice Literary Magazine, March
        2019

Title Index

I

J

L

M

N

O

First Line Index

U

www.ingramcontent.com/pod-product-compliance
Lightning Source LLC
Chambersburg PA
CBHW010857090426
42737CB00020B/3400